One-Minute Promises

STEVE MILLER

HARVEST HOUSE PUBLISHERS

EUGENE, OREGON

Cover Photo © Brian Hagiwara @ Brand X Images / Alamy

Cover by Terry Dugan Design, Minneapolis, Minnesota

ONE-MINUTE PROMISES
Copyright © 2006 by Steve Miller
Published by Harvest House Publishers
Eugene, Oregon 97402
www.harvesthousepublishers.com

ISBN-13: 978-0-7369-1761-2
ISBN-10: 0-7369-1761-6

Printed in the United States of America

06 07 08 09 10 11 12 13 / BP-MS / 12 11 10 9 8 7 6 5 4 3 2 1

There has not failed one word
of all His good promise.

1 KINGS 8:56

Contents

Love

O love of God, how strong and true!
Eternal and yet ever new;
Uncomprehended and unbought,
Beyond all knowledge and all thought.

HORATIUS BONAR

A Love That Never Diminishes

*God, who is rich in mercy, because of His great love
with which He loved us, even when we were dead
in trespasses, made us alive together with Christ.*

EPHESIANS 2:4-5

∞

Have you ever wondered, *How can God still want me
or love me after the ways I've failed Him?*

Yet God's mercy is so rich and His love is so great
that He loved you even when you were "dead in trespasses." Before you became a Christian, you were lost
in total spiritual darkness—you had nothing redeeming
to offer. Spiritually, you were utterly bankrupt. Even
then, in that depraved state, God reached out to you
in love and called you to Him in salvation so that you
might be made "alive together with Christ."

If He loved you even when you were at your
absolute worst as an unbeliever, then you can do
nothing as a believer that will diminish His love for
you. In fact, His love is not based on your performance.
Yes, you will grieve His heart when you sin. But you
can still count on His love for you, which is constant—
no matter what!

A Tough and Enduring Love

Yes, I have loved you with an everlasting love.

JEREMIAH 31:3

⌘

Though God gave this promise to ancient Israel, it has very definite significance to us today as well. The story behind this statement reminds us just how much God loves those He calls His own.

This promise came through the prophet Jeremiah, who warned the Israelites of God's anger and imminent punishment in response to their gross idolatry and other wicked practices. Even when God threatened severe judgment, He yearned for His people to repent, and affirmed His love for them.

Just as a parent still loves a rebellious child when punishing him, God loves us even when He must discipline us. We cannot outrun His love, for it is an everlasting love. May we never abuse it or take advantage of it, but rather thank Him for it and show Him our love in return.

A Love You Can Count On

I am persuaded that neither death nor life, nor angels nor principalities nor powers, nor things present nor things to come, nor height nor depth, nor any other created thing, shall be able to separate us from the love of God which is in Jesus Christ our Lord.

ROMANS 8:38-39

∽

God's love for us is so permanent, so indestructible, so everlasting that nothing—absolutely *nothing*—can separate us from it. This promise in Romans 8:38-39 is so all-encompassing that it has no exceptions whatsoever. Nothing can separate you and God.

Note what these verses don't promise. They don't tell us that God will help us to circumvent life's problems. They don't tell us that life is easier for those who are Christians. But God *does* promise He will be our constant companion through the hard times.

That's why, when trouble comes your way, you have nothing to fear. God is always at your side, ready to protect and care for you. Nothing will ever separate you from Him!

A Love That Never Changes

*For the mountains shall depart and the hills be
removed, but My kindness shall not depart from
you, nor shall My covenant of peace be removed.*

ISAIAH 54:10

∽

Though the earth may change and mountains disappear, God's love will never depart from His people. Though the forces of change are ever in motion all around us, God's kindness toward us remains constant. As the years pass by and time marches on, His promises to us are steadfast as ever.

God has pledged to love us with an enduring love. Nothing in the past, present, or future can alter that. Nothing will take His love or kindness away from you. What a comforting truth this is...we don't have to live in the fear that we have to earn His love or that we might inadvertently fall out of His favor. Have you expressed your appreciation to Him for this great and everlasting love?

Joy

Why should Christians be such a happy people?
It is good for our God;
it gives Him honor among men when we are glad.
It is good for us; it makes us strong....
It is good for the ungodly; when they see Christians glad,
they long to be believers themselves.
It is good for our fellow Christians;
it comforts them and tends to cheer them.

C.H. SPURGEON

The Source of True Joy

These things I have spoken to you, that my joy may remain in you, and that your joy may be full.

JOHN 15:11

∽

Christ desires that our joy "may be full." Not partial, not fleeting, but full.

The joy Jesus is speaking of is not a jolly cheerfulness. Rather, it is an inner happiness and contentment that doesn't depend on external circumstances. It is the assurance that God will use all that happens to us for our ultimate good and for His glory. And because it is internal, it isn't dependent on other people's actions or attitudes toward us.

Christ is the giver of joy, and the truths He taught—especially His promises—were given so that His joy might remain in us. The joy He gives is a kind that lasts, a kind that can buoy us upward when crises threaten to pull us downward.

Joy is not a matter of what's happening *around* you, but *inside* you. In your heart and mind, are you focused upon Jesus, His words, His promises? If you are, then you will know joy.

From Hindrance to Opportunity

*Count it all joy when you fall into various trials,
knowing that the testing of your faith produces patience.
But let patience have its perfect work, that you may be
perfect and complete, lacking nothing.*

JAMES 1:2-4

If we were to rank the seemingly most irrational statements in the Bible, this one would land near the top of the list. Count it all joy when life seems rotten? How can that possibly make sense?

But James is not talking about artificial smiles and giddy emotions that ignore our difficult circumstances. He's not saying we're to enjoy our trials or that they themselves are joy. Rather, he's saying we can have joy *in the midst* of our troubles. Joy that comes from knowing God is still in control. From knowing that hardships help to purify, strengthen, and mature us. From focusing on things that cannot be taken away from us rather than things that can.

When we view our troubles as opportunities, God can use us more effectively. Is that your heart's desire?

Strength

God is not waiting to show us strong in His behalf,
but Himself strong in our behalf.
That makes a lot of difference.
He is not out to demonstrate
what we can do but what He can do.

VANCE HAVNER

Waiting on the Lord

Wait on the LORD; be of good courage, and He shall strengthen your heart; wait, I say, on the LORD!

PSALM 27:14

తిత

Waiting on the Lord is hard to do in our instant age. At the touch of a keyboard, at the push of a button, we can have what we want. But not everything in life works like that. We still have concerns that remain unanswered, worries that have no immediate solutions. These stretch our patience and cause us to become anxious...worried...or even depressed or angry.

The psalmist who wrote, "Wait on the LORD" had faced the challenge of scanning the horizon of life and seeing nothing but dark and threatening storm clouds. His reply? Wait on the Lord. Be patient. After all, He can see into the future, beyond the horizon of our troubles, and we can't. He doesn't expect us to understand, but He invites us to trust Him and wait.

Let us not run ahead of God or act on our own power. Rather, let us wait and stay at His side...and He will strengthen us.

Waiting for the Best Possible Outcome

Those who wait for the LORD will gain new strength;
they will mount up with wings like eagles, they will run
and not get tired, they will walk and not become weary.

ISAIAH 40:31 (NASB)

❧

Noah waited 120 years for the flood. Abraham waited decades for his son Isaac. Hannah waited to the point of despair in her want of a son. Nehemiah and his fellow Israelites waited 70 years before their release from Babylon.

In every instance, those who waited on God saw wonderful results. Those who didn't wait made grave mistakes.

At times, waiting may seem the hardest thing in the world to do, but it's actually the easiest. For when we wait, we allow God the freedom to orchestrate our lives and circumstances in ways that bring about the very best possible outcome. Isn't that what we really want?

He Will Lift You Up

Do not fear, for I am with you; do not anxiously look
about you, for I am your God. I will strengthen you,
surely I will help you. Surely I will uphold you with
My righteous right hand.

ISAIAH 41:10 (NASB)

∽

What fears are you struggling with right now? What weighs heavily on your heart? Have you lifted your anxieties up to God and truly let go of them?

We may be weak and frail, but we have a strong and mighty God. He is so great and so powerful that He laid the foundations of the earth and determined the boundaries of the seas (Job 38:4,8), yet He never forgets to feed even the little birds that hunger for food (Matthew 6:26)

And God's promises in Isaiah 41:10 are absolute. They leave no room for exceptions:

I *am* your God.

I *will* strengthen you.

I *will* help you.

I *will* uphold you.

So when you find yourself being pulled down, look to God...and He will lift you up.

Nothing Is Too Hard

Is anything too hard for the LORD?

GENESIS 18:14

✍

How powerful is God?

Powerful enough to create the entire universe merely by speaking. To cover the entire globe in a flood. To part the Red Sea and close it up again. To feed and water two million Israelites every single day as they wandered through the wilderness for 40 years. To crumble the seemingly indomitable walls of Jericho with the sound of trumpets. To bring the Babylonian captivity to an end after 70 years, exactly as promised. To cause a virgin to give birth. To walk on water. To calm the violent winds and waves on the Sea of Galilee. To heal the blind, the deaf, the lame. To feed thousands from a few loaves of bread. To go to the cross with joy. And the crowning achievement on our behalf, to conquer the previously unconquerable grip of death.

Are you facing a situation too hard for you to handle? Give it to the Lord. Let Him take care of it. As we've just seen, nothing is too hard for Him.

Help in the Midst of Hardship

We are hard-pressed on every side, yet not crushed;
we are perplexed, but not in despair; persecuted,
but not forsaken; struck down, but not destroyed.

2 CORINTHIANS 4:8-9

∽

In every hardship we face, we can be absolutely certain God will preserve us. We may wonder about the limits of our endurance, but God promises never to let us reach the breaking point.

But why does God even allow us to face trials? Wouldn't we achieve more if we didn't have to struggle so much?

When all is well, we are much more likely to forget God. We have little or no reason to seek His help. But when the storms strike, we are compelled to draw closer to Him—which is where He wants us.

Someone once said, "Trials are not intended to break us but to make us." Difficulties *are* beneficial— they help us to grow stronger and wiser, and to plant our roots more deeply in the bedrock of God Himself.

Eternal Life

*One thought of eternity makes
all earthly sorrows fade away.*

BASILIA SCHLINK

The Best Guarantee Ever

*Most assuredly, I say to you, he who believes in Me
has everlasting life.*

JOHN 6:47

Almost nothing is 100 percent sure in life. Things
break. Time runs out. Investments go sour. Plans go
awry. People break promises. Weather changes. Friends
betray us. Loved ones hurt us. Coworkers don't follow
through. Our health deteriorates. Modern technology
doesn't stay modern. Tornadoes, hurricanes, floods,
and earthquakes destroy in an instant that which has
taken a lifetime to build.

But we Christians have one guarantee we can
always count on. It will never change. No one can ever
take it away from us. Nothing can ever happen to it.

That's the gift of eternal life. Eternal, as in forever
and ever. A perfect life, in the presence of a perfect
God, in the midst of perfect peace, perfect love, and
perfect joy.

Life's problems *will* come to an end. And someday,
we *will* enjoy eternal life.

It's guaranteed!

The Ultimate Makeover

If anyone is in Christ, he is a new creation; old things have passed away; behold, all things have become new.

2 CORINTHIANS 5:17

∽

Nothing is more radical than becoming a Christian. Believers have moved from death to life. From darkness to light. From rebellion to obedience. From despair to hope. From hatred to love. From turmoil to peace. From condemnation to acceptance. From hell to heaven.

Yes, the old things have passed away, and all things have become new. *All* things! You now have Christ, who promises to be with you always. You now have the Holy Spirit, who is your Counselor and Comforter. You have every single promise offered in God's Word—promises of protection, strength, wisdom, peace, deliverance, and victory. And you have everything that heaven has to offer—an eternal inheritance waiting for you. It's the ultimate makeover, the best package deal ever. And it's *all* given to *every* single Christian... including you!

An Accomplished Fact

Most assuredly, I say to you, he who hears My word and believes in Him who sent Me has everlasting life, and shall not come into judgment, but has passed from death into life.

JOHN 5:24

∽

In the song "It Is Well with My Soul," Horatio Gates Spafford wrote,

My sin—O, the bliss of this glorious thought—
My sin, not in part but the whole,
Is nailed to the cross and I bear it no more.
Praise the Lord, praise the Lord, O my soul!

Yes, *all* our sin was nailed to the cross. None of it condemns us anymore. We who are Christians *have* passed from death to life. Nothing can change the verdict. The phrase "has passed" is in the perfect tense, indicating an accomplished fact. We won't have any unexpected surprises regarding our destiny. After all, eternal life wouldn't be eternal if we could lose it.

How can we possibly thank God enough? As the song exclaims, "Praise the Lord, praise the Lord, O my soul!"

Forgiveness

Release! Signed in tears, sealed in blood,
written on heavy parchment,
recorded in eternal archives. The black ink
of the indictment is written all over
with the red ink of the cross:
"The blood of Jesus Christ cleanseth us from all sin."

T. DE WITT TALMAGE

Ready to Forgive

For you, Lord, are good, and ready to forgive, and abundant in mercy to all those who call upon You.

PSALM 86:5

~

Are you doubting whether God will really forgive you this time? After making yet the same mistake again? Perhaps you feel as if His patience with you has surely worn out by now.

But God is not like us human beings, who sometimes take sinister delight in withholding forgiveness from others. No, God is always "ready to forgive, and abundant in mercy." When we've wronged Him, He is eager for us to seek reconciliation with Him. He takes pleasure in our companionship and our dependence on Him. And it all starts by calling on Him—that is, turning away from that which offends Him.

Are you truly sorry? Do you desire for all to be right between you and Him? If your answer is yes, He will forgive you!

The Great Escape

In Him we have redemption through His blood, the forgiveness of sins, according to the riches of His grace.

EPHESIANS 1:7

∽

Imagine, for a moment, what life would be like if you had absolutely no choice but to spend eternity in hell. That would make life pretty bleak, wouldn't it? An utterly total absence of hope and joy. And an overwhelming sense of despair at being unable to reverse your downward descent toward an inescapable and horrible destiny.

Praise God—that's not the case! While we were totally helpless to escape the shackles of sin, Christ paid the required ransom for our release from bondage. He died so that we might live, and He became sin for us that we might become the righteousness of God in Him (2 Corinthians 5:21).

We have been redeemed and forgiven, and we have an incredible future to look forward to—thanks to His wonderful grace!

Gone!

As far as the east is from the west, so far has He removed our transgressions from us.

PSALM 103:12

⁓

When God forgives, He forgives so completely and so totally that we have no reason to ever return to the past and punish ourselves through feelings of guilt and regret. He has removed our transgressions "as far as the east is from the west." What does that mean?

Consider this: If you travel north, eventually you will reach the top of the globe, where you cannot help but start traveling south again. You can't travel north forever. Or south. But you *can* travel to the east or the west forever—and that's how far God has removed your sins from you.

Have you made a terrible mistake you just can't get over? If you've approached God with a sincerely repentant heart and asked Him for forgiveness, you have it already. The slate is wiped clean, the offense is gone forever.

Faithful to Forgive

If we confess our sins, He is faithful and just to forgive us our sins and to cleanse us from all unrighteousness.

1 JOHN 1:9

♫

We have a God who doesn't hold grudges. When we come to Him with a genuinely repentant heart asking for forgiveness, He doesn't say, "I need some time to think about it." No—His forgiveness is immediate, and His cleansing is whole.

And regardless of how great your sin is, God's forgiveness is greater. Don't make the mistake of thinking you've gone beyond the point of being forgivable. Don't accept Satan's invitation to throw a pity party for yourself or listen to his accusations that you have no hope and that you're unworthy of God's love.

As C.H. Spurgeon said, "You sin as a finite creature, but the Lord forgives as the infinite Creator." So don't let the past haunt you. Instead, live thankfully in God's forgiveness.

Amazing Grace

I, even I, am He who blots out your transgressions
for My own sake; and I will not remember your sins.

ISAIAH 43:25

&

God knows our hearts far better than we do. He knows our every fault, our every weakness. He knows the sins that have taken place in the deepest and most secret recesses of our minds and hearts. He knows every sin we have yet to commit in the future. He knows our entire rap sheet, from birth to death. We can hide nothing from Him.

And yet He still chose to extend the gift of salvation to us. He still chose to make forgiveness available through the Savior, Jesus Christ. In spite of our failures, He stands ready to blot them out and not remember them. No wonder we call this amazing grace!

As a Christian, be sure to never forget where you came from and how God has changed you. Won't you take a moment to thank Him now?

No Condemnation

*There is therefore now no condemnation to those who
are in Christ Jesus.*

ROMANS 8:1

∽

The Bible calls Satan "the accuser" (Revelation
12:10). And no wonder—he works overtime to make
us feel guilty about our past. "You're no good," he whis-
pers. "You call yourself a Christian? What about those
lustful thoughts in your mind? That gossip you helped
to spread? The lie you told at work?" And when you
do something *really* stupid, Satan gleefully chuckles,
"No way is God gonna forgive you for *that!*"

But your salvation was a gift given on the basis of
God's grace. You did nothing to obtain it, and you
cannot do anything to lose it. Once you're in Christ
Jesus, nothing can condemn you. He has paid for every
sin in your life—past, present, and future. So no one
can hold any sin against you—ever. Christ's sacrifice
covers it all.

So when you've already confessed a specific sin to
God and you're still haunted by it, don't pay attention
to Satan's accusations. God has forgiven you...so don't
withhold forgiveness from yourself!

Wisdom

Wisdom opens the eyes
both to the glories of heaven
and to the hollowness of earth.

J.A. MOTYER

The Great Counselor

I, wisdom....love those who love me, and those who
seek me diligently will find me.

PROVERBS 8:12,17

જી

Some decisions are simple and don't require much thought. And when we just can't make up our minds, we'll flip a coin or let a friend make the choice for us.

But occasionally we face decisions of greater significance—those that require a lot of us or have a long-term consequence. Should we, or shouldn't we? Which is the better of two options? Sometimes we'll vacillate to the point of agony, unsure of what to do.

When we can't make up our minds, or we're just not sure, we have no better Counselor to go to than God Himself. Proverbs 2:6 says, "The LORD gives wisdom; from His mouth come knowledge and understanding." When you have a decision to make, bring it to Him and leave it at His feet. Keep it before Him in prayer and ask Him to lead you. His perfect and infinite wisdom is more than adequate for even the biggest decisions we face.

Unlimited Wisdom

*If any of you lacks wisdom, let him ask of God,
who gives to all liberally and without reproach,
and it will be given to him.*

JAMES 1:5

❧

If we lack wisdom? Given a choice between human wisdom and divine, we should rush to our knees in perpetual prayer for the latter!

God puts no limit to the wisdom we can ask for. Rather, He "gives to all liberally." We can never cry out to Him too many times. God is not the stern schoolmaster who barks, "When will you ever learn?" Rather, He is the patient Father who says, "I'm glad you asked!"

James 1:5 refers to wisdom in the context of life's trials. Too often we see our problems as hindrances. But they're actually opportunities to seek wisdom. And in the very act of asking, we draw ourselves closer to God—yet another benefit of experiencing troubles.

God asks no price for His priceless wisdom. It's free. Simply ask...and He will give.

Peace

Peace comes not from the absence of troubles,
but from the presence of God.

ALEXANDER MACLAREN

Our Source of Peace

*You will keep him in perfect peace, whose mind is
stayed on You, because he trusts in You.*

ISAIAH 26:3

∽

The opposite of peace is anxiety. We usually experience anxiety when we're uncertain about the future, concerned about meeting our needs, or faced with danger. And when we allow worries to eat away at us, we are failing to trust God to carry us through.

To really trust God means to believe that He can see into the future and that nothing will take Him by surprise. To believe that He knows our every need and will provide. To believe that His power is greater than any danger that might threaten us.

Do you believe? Is your mind "stayed" on God—in other words, is your trust fixed on Him constantly? If so, then you will know "perfect peace." You will know the freedom that comes from totally resting in God and trusting Him to care for you.

Which Will You Choose?

The LORD will give strength to His people; the LORD will bless His people with peace.

PSALM 29:11

∾

When troubles first come along, our inclination is to tackle them head-on without giving much thought to asking God for help. Not until they get worse and overwhelm us do we cry out to our heavenly Father in despair. Instead of looking to Him at the first instant, we turn to Him only as a last resort.

Why do we attempt to rely on human weakness when we can call on divine strength? Why do we exhaust ourselves through worry when we can have peace? We can choose between fighting the stormy seas on our own or resting in the harbor of His strength and peace.

At the first hint of trouble, flee to God. Psalm 29:11 promises that He *will* give you strength and He *will* bless you with peace.

Peace Even in the Midst of Chaos

Peace I leave with you, My peace I give to you....
Let not your heart be troubled, neither let it be
afraid.

JOHN 14:27

∽

Jesus spoke these words to the disciples shortly before leaving them. He knew that their world would soon turn upside down and that they would be filled with fear in response to His crucifixion and His departure to return to the Father. He encouraged them, in advance of this tumultuous upheaval, not to be afraid but to rest in His peace.

One of the many names for Jesus in the Bible is "Prince of Peace" (Isaiah 9:6). Someday, He will return to earth and establish His kingdom of peace. Yet we don't need to wait until then to know His peace. He offers it to us right now in the midst of life's chaos and crises. He promised, "I am with you always, even to the end of the age" (Matthew 28:20). Because He is present within us, His peace is constantly available to us...and we need only to ask Him for it.

Exchanging Worry for Peace

Be anxious for nothing, but in everything by prayer and supplication, with thanksgiving, let your requests be made known to God; and the peace of God, which surpasses all understanding, will guard your hearts and minds through Christ Jesus.

PHILIPPIANS 4:6-7

∽

What an incredible offer—our worries in exchange for God's peace! It's actually more than an offer; it's a command. When we worry, we are doubting God—we are questioning His ability to control the outcome of our circumstances, His timing, His ability to care for us and intervene on our behalf.

Worry cannot change a thing. But God can. That's why our heavenly Father lovingly encourages us to yield all our cares to Him. He doesn't call us to understand, but rather to trust. And when we surrender our concerns to Him, He will fill us with a peace that calms us, lifts us above the turmoils of life, and tells a watching world, "My God is a mighty God, and He will carry me through this."

A Trust That Leads to Peace

*Great peace have those who love Your law, and
nothing causes them to stumble.*

PSALM 119:165

∽

When we have a true love for God's Word, we will
know true peace. When we rest in the commands and
assurances of Scripture, we will experience rest in our
hearts.

On a human level, when we love someone, we
believe what they say and we *trust* what they do. We
have *confidence* that person has our best interests at
heart.

Do you believe what God says about the afflictions
of life and how they can strengthen us? Do you trust
Him in both good times and bad? Do you have confidence that *all* things work together for good, and not
just some? Can you accept the hard sayings of Scripture without question?

If you can answer yes, you will have peace and not
stumble. May we seek to not only read and understand
God's Word but also love and believe it!

Peace in the Storm

He who dwells in the shelter of the Most High will rest in the shadow of the Almighty. I will say of the LORD, "He is my refuge and my fortress, my God, in whom I trust."

PSALM 91:1-2 (NIV)

⁓

We live in a stormy world. We're surrounded by the raging seas and violent winds of broken relationships, workplace pressures, and difficult circumstances. We grow weary as we struggle to endure in the midst of anxiety, discouragement, and hurt. At times we may feel as if the storm has become a hurricane, and nothing is going right. We want to escape it all, but so incessant are the rains and squalls that we lose hope.

At times like these, we can look to the promise that when we seek shelter in God, we can rest in His shadow. He is our refuge, our hiding place. He is our fortress, our shield of protection. He is the quiet harbor in which we can find true peace. When life seems to spin out of control, we can find security in knowing He has complete control over life itself. He doesn't ask us to understand our circumstances; He asks only that we trust Him.

Security

Security is not the absence of danger
but the presence of God,
no matter what the danger.

ANONYMOUS

The Certainty of Future Glory

For whom He foreknew, He also predestined to be conformed to the image of His Son....Moreover whom He predestined, these He also called; whom He called, these He also justified; and whom He justified, these he also glorified.

ROMANS 8:29-30

෴

Did you notice that the very last word in Romans 8:30—the word *glorified*—is in the past tense?

If you're a Christian, these verses describe you. You have been predestined, called, and justified, and you will be glorified. So definite is this last fact that the apostle Paul wrote it in the past tense even though it hasn't happened yet.

These words are a wonderful testimony of how secure we are in Christ. From the time we were predestined—before the foundation of the world, according to Ephesians 1:4-5—to the time we are glorified in heaven, we are firmly in God's grasp. Not a single one of us will be lost somewhere along the way. As Jesus said in John 10:29, no one is able to snatch us out of the Father's hand. We have nothing to fear; our place in heaven is secure.

A Strong Tower

You have been a shelter for me, a strong tower from the enemy.

PSALM 61:3

∽

In Bible times, people built towers along city walls to help stabilize them and to provide a city's residents with places of defense and refuge. Towers, then, had a key role in protecting cities and their inhabitants from marauding enemies.

But a tower was effective only as long as people stayed within its strong walls. Those who wandered away did so at their own risk and became extremely vulnerable targets.

God is our tower, and as long as we remain in His shelter—by staying near to Him, living in obedience to Him, fleeing to Him instead of away from Him when we are tempted—we will have His protection.

The enemy can't defeat us unless we make ourselves vulnerable. God has promised you protection, and *nothing* has the power to thwart His care for you.

An Ever-Attentive Father

*The eyes of the LORD are on the righteous, and His
ears are open to their prayers.*

1 PETER 3:12

☙

It happens more often than you like to recount. As
you first wake up, you're already overwhelmed by the
burden of the many responsibilities demanding your
attention. You have more than enough troubles and
not enough time. You wonder how you're going to
make it through the day.

When we're at our busiest, we are most in need of
a few quiet moments to give the day to God. We need
to set aside our self-sufficiency and ask for His super-
natural strength. To yield our anxiety and ask for His
peace. And to lift our concerns to Him rather than sup-
press them within.

God is watching over you, and He's ready to hear
you. With His help, you can make it through the day.
He will enable you to accomplish what you need to get
done. Rest in Him...and your day will go much better.

Treasures Waiting in Heaven for You

[You have] an inheritance incorruptible and unde-filed and that does not fade away, reserved in heaven for you.

1 PETER 1:4

❧

Chances are, you've lived long enough to know the pain that comes from the loss of a possession you dearly treasured. And you've seen that the things of earth do not last forever. They wear out, break down, or get lost or stolen. And someday, when you die, the riches you worked so hard to acquire will end up in the hands of others. You can't take anything with you to heaven.

Yet you are rich with spiritual possessions that are waiting for you in heaven at this very moment. Among them are God Himself, the Lord Jesus Christ, eternal life, and perfect and everlasting rest, joy, and peace. These "possessions" will never rust or be destroyed. They can never be stolen, nor will they fade away with the passage of time.

Earthly riches don't last; heavenly riches do. To which are you devoting your attention?

Forever Secure

I give [my sheep] eternal life, and they shall never perish; no one can snatch them out of my hand. My Father, who has given them to me, is greater than all; no one can snatch them out of my Father's hand

JOHN 10:28-29 (NIV)

~

Here we find four great promises for believers: 1) We possess eternal life, 2) we will never perish, 3) no one can snatch us out of God's hand, and 4) God is greater than all. Note that Jesus repeats the promise that no one can take us away. We are forever secure in the hands of both Jesus and the Father.

If you've ever been anxious that somehow you might lose your salvation, worry no more. Because God is "greater than all," nothing is powerful enough to loosen us from His grip. Because we "shall never perish," nothing can steal our assurance that we will one day live in God's presence forever.

Satan wants us to doubt our eternal security so that we live in fear and trepidation. But God has proclaimed His promises to us so we can live in confidence and joy.

Becoming a Finished Masterpiece

I thank my God...being confident of this very thing,
that He who has begun a good work in you will com-
plete it until the day of Jesus Christ.

PHILIPPIANS 1:3,6

∽

How many projects have you started but never gotten around to finishing? In every case, you undoubtedly started out with the best of intentions. But eventually, for one reason or another, the projects went to the wayside.

At the moment of your salvation, God began a project in you. He desires for you to grow spiritually mature and become more like Christ. This transformation is ongoing for the rest of your life. At no step along the way will God set you aside or give up on you. His work in you will continue every moment of every day. You might not notice the growth, but He promises that He *will* nurture you and that He *will* carry that work to completion. And by the time you enter eternity, you will be a finished masterpiece.

He Enables, We Enjoy

Now to Him who is able to keep you from stumbling, and to present you faultless before the presence of His glory with exceeding joy...be glory and majesty, dominion and power.

JUDE 24-25

Are you giving all the credit where it's due?

Whatever you are able to do in the Christian life, you can do because of God—because of His empowerment, His wisdom, His strength, His everything. He is the One who keeps us from falling, and He enables us to stand in righteousness. Because of what He did through Jesus Christ, we will live in His presence someday and experience eternal bliss.

When you find yourself taking credit for an accomplishment, don't forget who really made it possible. And when others praise you for a job well done, pass that same praise along to God. *He* is the One who enables you. And yet He graciously allows you to fully enjoy the benefits that result from His work in you!

Deliverance

Fear not, I am with thee; O be not dismayed,
For I am thy God and will still give thee aid;
I'll strengthen thee, help thee, and cause thee to stand,
Upheld by my righteous omnipotent hand.

FROM THE HYMN "HOW FIRM A FOUNDATION"

Victory Is Always Possible

He who is in you is greater than he who is in the world.

1 JOHN 4:4

∾

Satan is a tireless foe. He is thoroughly committed to making life as difficult as possible for God's children, throwing every weapon he has in our path in the hopes of hindering us or causing us to stumble. Though he knows he can never have us back, he figures he may as well render us as ineffective as possible.

But we have no reason to be afraid, for Satan is a finite, created being, and we belong to the infinite, almighty Creator God who is all-powerful, all-knowing, and all-present. By contrast, Satan has none of those attributes. He's no match against God.

Yes, the battles we face may become fierce at times. But the Lord who won a decisive and permanent victory at the cross is the same Lord who lives in our hearts. And because He dwells in us, He can help us prevail against the one who is in the world.

A Loyal Protection

The eyes of the LORD run to and fro throughout the whole earth, to show Himself strong on behalf of those whose heart is loyal to Him.

2 CHRONICLES 16:9

∽

In ages past, the role of a king was to protect his loyal subjects. However, if a citizen chose to rebel against the king or journey outside the boundaries of the kingdom, the king's promise of protection no longer applied.

We find a similar promise in the Bible: Those who are loyal to God can count on His protective care. If a problem arises in your life, God is aware of it. No crisis, no tragedy in your life will ever catch God off guard. He sees all and knows all. And regardless of how overwhelming your problem is, it cannot overwhelm God.

For the moment, you may find yourself forced to your knees in dependence on the Lord and crying out in prayer, but ultimately, God will bring deliverance. When we remain loyal to God, He will remain loyal to us—with a fierce tenacity that will carry us to victory.

More than Conquerors

In all these things we are more than conquerors through Him who loved us.

ROMANS 8:37

❧

The Bible says that we who are Christians are more than conquerors...*through Him.*

Perhaps the most significant sense in which we are conquerors is that we can resist temptation and sin. Before salvation, we had no choice. But in Christ, we can refuse to yield the parts of our bodies as "instruments of unrighteousness" and instead present them as "instruments of righteousness" (Romans 6:13).

You can overcome your anger...through Him. Your lust...through Him. Your covetousness...through Him. Your bitterness...through Him. Your victory over any kind of sin is possible only because of Christ's victory on the cross. To mortify your sin, you must go to Him who mortified sin at Calvary.

Do you want to be more than a conqueror? Go to Him. He has already secured the victory for you.

Making the Impossible Possible

Be strong and of good courage, do not fear nor be afraid of them; for the LORD your God, He is the One who goes with you. He will not leave you nor forsake you.

DEUTERONOMY 31:6

∽

This was God's command to the nation of Israel before they crossed the Jordan into the Promised Land. The Israelites were about to face huge armies that had powerful weapons, and God wanted the people of Israel to place their confidence in Him—not in themselves or their woefully inadequate fighting gear.

When we face an overwhelming challenge, our initial response is often discouragement or fear. But even if defeat seems certain, remember this: That which seems impossible to us is always possible with God.

He stands before us in the battle, taking the enemy's blows and clearing a safe path on which we can follow. He will never withdraw His help, and though the heat of the fighting may cause us to momentarily waver or stumble, ultimately, victory belongs to the Lord—and to us.

Deliverance from Temptation

No temptation has overtaken you except such as is common to man; but God is faithful, who will not allow you to be tempted beyond what you are able, but with the temptation will also make the way of escape, that you may be able to bear it.

1 CORINTHIANS 10:13

❧

One key reason we look forward to living in heaven is that we won't have to struggle against temptation anymore.

But while we're still on this earth, we can take great comfort in the two guarantees found in 1 Corinthians 10:13: We will *never* experience a temptation greater than we can resist, and God will *always* provide a way of escape.

The spiritual power you have within you is greater than any temptation that might attempt to seduce you. "The Lord is faithful, and He will strengthen and protect you from the evil one" (2 Thessalonians 3:3 NASB).

When you are tempted, do you succumb to the temporary satisfaction sin offers? Or do you run to the Lord for strength to resist? The power is available...you must choose whether you use it.

Waiting with Open Arms

Let us therefore come boldly to the throne of grace,
that we may obtain mercy and find grace to help in
time of need.

HEBREWS 4:16

∽

At the time these words were written, the concept of approaching a king's throne boldly was radical. People just didn't do that. People approached kings with trepidation and fear because displeasing them, even slightly, could mean death.

Yet God, who sits on the highest and most powerful throne of all, is the humblest and most approachable King of all. Earthly rulers might hold their subjects at a distance with disdain, but the heavenly Ruler welcomes His children affectionately with love.

Hebrews 4:16 was written in the context of temptation. Are you struggling? Are you embarrassed or reluctant to call to the Lord for help? Rest assured, no grace can exceed His; no mercy can surpass His. You have no better place to go for help than to Him. So when temptation strikes, *run* to Him. He's waiting with open arms.

Nothing to Fear

"Oh Death, where is your sting? O Hades, where is your victory?" The sting of death is sin, and the strength of sin is the law. But thanks be to God, who gives us the victory through our Lord Jesus Christ

1 CORINTHIANS 15:55-57

&

Because of Jesus Christ's work on the cross and in the resurrection, death no longer has the power to end your life. Death is no longer the permanent silencer; rather, God has permanently silenced it.

What's more, for the Christian, death is not the end but the beginning. It's the start of life without affliction, without pain, without temptation, without sin. Death removes us from the land of the dying and takes us to the land of the living.

While the apostle Paul was in prison facing possible death, he proclaimed that "to die is gain" (Philippians 1:21). He then said he had "a desire to depart and be with Christ, which is far better" (verse 23).

Truly, the believer has no reason to fear death. Thanks to Christ, tragedy has turned to triumph, and mortality has turned to immortality. What a victory indeed!

Help in Every Affliction

Many are the afflictions of the righteous, but the Lord *delivers him out of them all.*

PSALM 34:19

∽

The word "many" in that verse isn't very comforting, is it? We can expect *numerous* afflictions. Persecution, trials, and troubles are guaranteed in this world. Knowing that, we cannot help but wonder: If God promises to deliver us, then why do we experience affliction in the first place?

Our Father's promise of deliverance does not mean He will remove us from life's problems altogether. Rather, He will *preserve* us through them. Though we may suffer scratches and bruises, we will not be destroyed. Though we may endure loneliness and misunderstandings, we will not be forsaken. Though we can be certain of difficulties, we can be equally certain God will help us in *every* affliction, for He promises to deliver us "out of them *all*." And the ultimate deliverance is still ahead of us—our journey home to heaven, where we will never experience affliction again.

Power

Surely our greatest trouble in the Christian life is our failure to realize that God is not as man. The greatest sin of every Christian, and the Christian Church in general, is to limit the eternal, absolute power of God to the measure of our own minds and concepts and understandings.

MARTYN LLOYD-JONES

The Source for a Productive Life

I am the vine, you are the branches. He who abides in Me, and I in him, bears much fruit; for without Me you can do nothing.

JOHN 15.5

&

Deep within our nature is a desire to have a real and significant purpose in life. And when we become Christians, that desire becomes more refined—we want to live productively for God and bear fruit for His kingdom.

The secret to such fruitfulness is remarkably simple, yet it requires discipline. Jesus promised that when we abide in Him, we will bear "much fruit." To abide implies intimacy, closeness, a constant pursuing after. Do you draw near to Him daily? Do you spend time in His Word? Do you yield yourself completely to Him? This is all that He asks—He doesn't require us to have a theology degree or years of training. He doesn't expect us to bear fruit in our own power. He produces all the results. We need only to remain close to Him so He can work through us.

Freedom from Fear

*God has not given us a spirit of fear, but of power
and of love and of a sound mind.*

2 TIMOTHY 1:7

∽

If you are facing a trial or threat that has instilled fear in your heart, that fear didn't come from God. He has given you everything you need to respond effectively to whatever comes your way in life.

You have power: Ephesians 3:20 says He "is able to do exceedingly abundantly above all that we ask or think, according to the power that works in us."

You have love: the kind of love that does not lash out in anger or vengeance toward the people or circumstances who have caused your fear. "Love your enemies, bless those who curse you, do good to those who hate you, and pray for those who spitefully use you and persecute you" (Matthew 5:44).

You have a sound mind: with the help of the Spirit and the Word, you can respond in a clearheaded manner rather than with confusion. "If any of you lacks wisdom, let him ask of God" (James 1:5).

74

Companionship

The soul that on Jesus hath leaned for repose,
I will not, I will not desert to his foes,
That soul, though all hell should endeavor to shake,
I'll never, no never, no never forsake.

FROM THE HYMN "HOW FIRM A FOUNDATION"

Always Near

He Himself has said, "I will never leave you nor for-sake you."

HEBREWS 13:5

∾

Have you felt distant from the Lord lately? Or wondered if He's even listening to your prayers? If so, you don't need to worry that God has moved away or abandoned you. Your emotions or thoughts may betray you and tell you He's far away, but the Bible assures us He's as near as He's ever been.

So emphatic is this promise that the original Greek text contains multiple negatives. Together, they drive home the point that for God to ever leave us is absolutely impossible.

When life doesn't go our way, we may find ourselves wanting to give up on God, to shut Him out of our lives. Fortunately, God will never return the favor. He will remain faithful to us. May we never for a moment want to stray away from Him!

His Devotion to You

Draw near to God and He will draw near to you.

JAMES 4:8

✍

How easily we are distracted from God! When we pray, our minds wander far from spiritual matters. When we attempt to read His Word regularly, we allow ourselves to be pulled away by "urgent" tasks that "must" get done. Though we know our true treasures are in heaven, we oftentimes become more preoccupied with the riches of earth. And when temptation beckons us, instead of fleeing toward God, we linger, not really wanting to say no to the bait dangling before us.

The verses preceding James 4:8 mention those who seek friendship with the world and the fulfillment of their own pleasures. But God jealously yearns for the devotion of those who are His own...and James 4:8 stands as a promise that when we come back to Him with a genuine desire to seek and submit to Him alone, He will welcome us with open arms.

Have you been a wandering sheep lately? Do you need to come back to a closer walk with the Good Shepherd? Draw near to Him, and He will draw near to you.

At Your Side

*When you pass through the waters, I will be with
you; and through the rivers, they shall not overflow
you. When you walk through the fire, you shall not
be burned, nor shall the flame scorch you.*

ISAIAH 43:2

∽

One of the unfortunate myths that has persisted
among believers is that life as a Christian is supposed
to be free of problems and pain. But the Bible never
says that. Here, we read that we will pass through the
waters and rivers, through the fire and flames.

But as we do, God promises to be with us and that
nothing will completely overtake us. We may struggle
against the swift current of life or even stumble into the
water, but we'll never drown. We may feel the intense
heat of life's trials, but they will never destroy us. God
will enable us to survive through every peril till that day
of final redemption. That is why the psalmist could say
with confidence, "The LORD is on my side, I will not
fear" (Psalm 118:6).

Feeling Special

I am with you always, even to the end of the age.

MATTHEW 28:20

∽

We often envy those who have the rare fortune to know a famous person. And yet as a Christian, you have a personal relationship with the King of kings and Lord of lords Himself. Talk about connections!

And each word of His promise to you in Matthew 28:20 is packed with incredible truth:

I—Jesus Himself, not a stand-in or substitute

am—as in *really* and *right now* with you—not maybe or possibly

with—He's closer than a friend or brother and will never desert you.

you—You're the one! He cares about *you.*

always—every single moment, every single day... from now till eternity

Indeed, His name is Immanuel, which means "God with us." Not symbolically, but literally. *He* made that choice. Doesn't that make you feel pretty special?

Goodness

It is not enough that we acknowledge
God's infinite resources; we must believe also
that He is infinitely generous to bestow them.

A.W. TOZER

A Perfect Father

*To all who received him, to those who believed in his
name, he gave the right to become children of God.*

JOHN 1:12 (NIV)

⟳

Human parents who love their children do everything they can to meet their needs and oftentimes make
personal sacrifices for them. And the same is true about
God, to an even greater extent: He promises to meet
our every true need, and He made an enormous personal sacrifice on our behalf—one that no one could
ever match.

Maybe at times you've doubted God's goodness.
But consider the contrast the Bible makes between
human parents and our heavenly Parent: "If you then,
being evil [that is, imperfect and fallen], know how to
give good gifts to your children, how much more will
your Father who is in heaven give good things to those
who ask Him!" (Matthew 7:11).

God is a perfect Father who cares for His children
with a perfect love. And we are His beloved. Have you
noticed the fatherly care He has shown to you today?

Two Constant Companions

Surely goodness and mercy shall follow me all the days of my life; and I will dwell in the house of the LORD *forever.*

PSALM 23:6

℘

On every single day of our journey toward heaven, we have two constant companions: God's goodness and His mercy. Because of His goodness the apostle Paul could say, "My God shall supply *all* your need according to His riches" (Philippians 4:19). And because of His mercy we can say, "There is therefore now no condemnation to those who are in Christ Jesus" (Romans 8:1).

God gives all that we need (that's His goodness), and He takes away all our sins (that's His mercy). He is our abundant Provider and our able Protector. He sustains us and sanctifies us. And because He is forever faithful, His goodness and mercy will continue without fail...forever.

The Proof of His Love

The LORD is good, a stronghold in the day of trouble.

NAHUM 1:7

∾

Many of the troubles we face in life are beyond our comprehension. "Why did God allow that?" we ask. "What good can possibly come from this?" When tough questions like these arise, we can take consolation in a powerful truth repeated all through the Bible: *The Lord is good.*

God is gracious, merciful, and compassionate. He has confirmed this again and again by His past goodness to us. When the psalmist was deeply troubled, he asked, "Has God forgotten to be gracious?" He then answered his own question by saying, "I will remember the works of the LORD; surely I will remember your wonders of old" (77:9,11).

Need encouragement? First, look back. Fill your mind with thoughts of God's goodness to you in the past. Then look ahead...and rest assured in the truth that His goodness will continue into the future.

Hope

Hope can see heaven through the thickest clouds.

THOMAS BROOKS

Growing More like Christ

We know that when He is revealed, we shall be like Him, for we shall see Him as He is.

1 JOHN 3:2

೮೧

While we Christians are here on earth, we will never resolve "the great tension": We are forgiven and cleansed children of God, and yet we still struggle with and succumb to sin. From a *positional* standpoint, God has declared us fully righteous, but from a *practical* standpoint, we still exhibit from time to time the unrighteous ways of man. The tension between our position and our practice won't disappear until our mortal bodies are changed to immortal ones.

In the meantime, the Holy Spirit is shaping us to become more like Christ. Sometimes this "sculpting" process is slow and painful. We become impatient, wishing for results more quickly. But we read that one day "we shall be like Him," and "He who has begun a good work in you will complete it" (Philippians 1:6).

When you arrive on heaven's shore, both your position and practice will match perfectly. And that's a harmony you will know *forever*.

Forging Good from Bad

We know that all things work together for good to those who love God.

ROMANS 8:28

∽

Romans 8:28 is perhaps one of the most oft-quoted verses in the Bible...and one of the more frequently misunderstood.

What it's not saying: It's not saying *all* things are good. It's not saying that bad things will somehow *become* good. And it's not saying our lives will be free of trouble, always filled with good.

What it is saying: God has the power to somehow, in ways we don't understand, take the challenges, the difficulties, and the pains of life and forge beautiful results from them. These results can include greater patience, stronger faith, deeper trust, purer motives, truer humility, nobler desires, and a more God-centered life.

Bad will still happen. But somewhere, somehow, good can come from it. That's God's promise to those who love Him.

Lift Up Your Eyes

I will lift up my eyes to the hills—from whence comes my help? My help comes from the LORD, who made heaven and earth.

PSALM 121:1-2

∽

When troubles come, Satan wants us to look downward and inward. He wants us to keep our eyes on our problems, our worries, our sorrows. He wants us to try to climb out of the slippery pit of despair using our own feeble resources.

True help, however, comes only from above. When we need strength, we should seek out someone who is stronger than we are. The answer, then, is to look upward and outward—to look beyond our feeble selves to the Almighty Creator of heaven and earth. He has put His power at our disposal!

And when you lift up your eyes, you'll find your heart lifted up as well—with the hope and comfort that comes from knowing that no crisis is too great for God to handle.

A Savior You Can Count On

Jesus Christ is the same yesterday, today, and forever.

HEBREWS 13:8

∽

If you can count on anyone, Jesus Christ is the One. Because He is perfect, He does not need to change. And because He is faithful, He will not change.

Consider what this means to you: He will never change His mind about your salvation. Retract the forgiveness extended to you. Alter the requirements for getting to heaven. Void any of His promises to you. Negate the spiritual inheritance awaiting you in eternity. Withdraw His presence from you. Diminish in His ability to preserve you, provide for you, and protect you.

In a world full of people and circumstances that change from one moment to the next, the truth that Jesus is always the same is a wonderful source of security. While the winds of change swirl all around us, we can stand firm in the fact that Jesus is the same yesterday, today, and forever.

The Power of Belief

Why are you cast down, O my soul? And why are
you disquieted within me? Hope in God.

PSALM 43:5

❧

The ride on the train of discouragement, disappointment, and depression always descends a steep slope. How can we put on the brakes and stop this descent? The psalmist tells us the solution is to "hope in God."

The Puritan writer Richard Sibbes said that "the nature of hope is to expect that which faith believes." Do you believe God is powerful enough to change your circumstances? Do you believe He can use the negative situations of life to bring about positive results in you? Do you believe He loves you so much that even when hope seems to have died, deliverance *will* come?

When the darkness surrounds you, remember what God can do. Don't give up, for no storm lasts forever. Eventually the clouds will clear, and the sun will shine.

Do you believe? If you do, faith will give birth to hope...and turn your descent around into an ascent marked by confidence, peace, and joy.

Faithfulness

*When we trustfully resign ourselves,
and all our affairs into God's hands,
fully persuaded of His love and faithfulness,
the sooner shall we be satisfied
with His providence and realize that
"He doeth all things well."*

A.W. PINK

A Guaranteed Protection

The LORD is faithful, and he will strengthen and protect you from the evil one.

2 THESSALONIANS 3:3 (NIV)

∽

One characteristic that truly sets God apart from people is that He is *faithful*. What He says, He will do—without hesitation, equivocation, or compromise. Neither the passage of time, nor changes in circumstances, nor those who oppose Him with all their might can undermine the certainty that the Lord will follow through.

God is faithful to keep His promises (Deuteronomy 7:9), to carry our salvation to completion (1 Thessalonians 5:24), to provide a way of escape from temptation (1 Corinthians 10:13), and as the verse at the top of this page says, to strengthen and protect us from Satan.

This means we have no reason to fear our greatest adversary. God is faithful; He *will* protect us. What a wonderful assurance! Yet we must still do our part—which is to "submit to God. Resist the devil" (James 4:7).

His Pledge to You

He who calls you is faithful, who also will do it.

1 THESSALONIANS 5:24

∞

In the verse above, what has God promised to be faithful to do? The previous verse gives us the answer: "May the God of peace Himself sanctify you completely; and may your whole spirit, soul, and body be preserved blameless at the coming of our Lord Jesus Christ."

So God not only gives salvation to us as a free gift but also works within us to make us pure. He doesn't say, "Okay, I've saved you from sin. Now it's up to you to stay holy." As 2 Peter 1:3 says, "His divine power has given to us all things that pertain to life and godliness." God doesn't stop at commanding us to obey Him; He gives us the resources that enable us to do what He asks.

And why does God do this? Because He is faithful. He has made a pledge to preserve us till Jesus returns, and He will keep it. Aren't you glad you don't have to count on your own faithfulness?

Sufficiency

*You may never know that Jesus is all you need,
until Jesus is all you have.*

CORRIE TEN BOOM

All Sufficiency in All Things

God loves a cheerful giver. And God is able to make all grace abound toward you, that you, always having all sufficiency in all things, may have an abundance for every good work.

2 CORINTHIANS 9:7-8

∾

In the manner that you give to others, God will give to you. As you give generously and with discernment to those who have need, God will replenish your supply so that you yourself are never in need. He is "able to make *all grace abound*"—that is, His grace is infinite...so that you will have "*all* sufficiency in *all* things." The repeated use of the qualifier "all" should forever settle in our minds that we will never lack what we truly need.

So ask God to bring to your attention those who have need...and as He does, give generously, knowing that through your actions, you will give others a glimpse of God's abounding goodness. Give cheerfully to others...and God's grace will overflow to you!

Every Good Gift

*My God shall supply all your need according to His
riches in glory by Christ Jesus.*

PHILIPPIANS 4:19

∽

God knows our needs before we ask Him. But
sometimes we insist on being self-sufficient and fulfilling our needs in our own power, forgetting or even
refusing to go to the Lord and ask. Not until we ask
does He bless—James 4:2 says, "You do not have
because you do not ask." God desires for us to acknowledge our dependence on Him and recognize Him as the
sole source of "every good gift and every perfect gift"
(James 1:17).

And when God gives, He does so "according to His
riches." He provides for us not merely in a token
manner but in proportion to His infinite abundance.
The result? Our true needs are fully met. He does this
because He cares for us, loves us, delights in us, and
promises to be faithful to us.

Total Dependence

Not that we are sufficient of ourselves to think of anything as being from ourselves, but our sufficiency is from God.

2 CORINTHIANS 3:5

⁊

Do you realize you can never be too dependent upon God? In fact, He desires that you be fully dependent upon Him—that you ask for His wisdom, strength, and provision in even the smallest details of your life.

The world we live in teaches us to be self-sufficient—to pull up our own bootstraps, to face up to life's challenges, to not buckle under when the going gets tough. We've been so conditioned by this kind of thinking that we hesitate to make our needs known to our brothers and sisters in Christ, and even to God Himself.

You bring God great pleasure when you place your responsibilities, your decisions, your dreams, your family, your possessions—everything great and small—at His feet, asking Him to guide your every step in every matter. The more you depend upon Him, the more He is able to bless you!

Letting God's Power Shine

I can do all things through Christ who strengthens me.

PHILIPPIANS 4:13

∽

Without God's power, Gideon's army of 300 would never have defeated an enemy of 10,000. When David slew Goliath, he placed his confidence in God, not a suit of armor. And as long as Peter looked to Christ, he was able to walk on water. But the moment he glanced downward, he sank.

All through the Bible, we see this important truth again and again: Without God's help, we are nothing. But when we depend wholly on Him...watch out!

Regardless of the difficulty of the circumstance, God will enable you to rise to the occasion. You may experience great pain or heartache. You may struggle with uncertainty or discouragement. Yet such is beneficial, for in our trials, God's power has the opportunity to shine all the more. Do not worry, for God will never fail you.

A Sufficient Grace

*My grace is sufficient for you, for My strength is
made perfect in weakness.*

2 CORINTHIANS 12:9

❧

Can you imagine God turning down a prayer
request from one of the greatest leaders in the New
Testament, the apostle Paul? A request made not once,
not twice, but three times? Paul doesn't tell us what
bothered him. But it must have been serious, for he
"pleaded with the Lord three times." And God's
response? "No...My grace is sufficient for you."

God knew He could accomplish more by showing
His power through Paul's weakness than by removing
Paul's weakness altogether. Is that how you view the
hardships in your life? Have you considered that you
might actually receive greater benefit by persevering
through your weaknesses than by not having them at all?

Without our afflictions, we would not be intimately
acquainted with God's grace and strength. In this sense
we can truly be thankful for our trials...for each one is
yet another opportunity for our all-sufficient God to
display His strength in us and through us.

Every Spiritual Blessing

Blessed be the God and Father of our Lord Jesus Christ, who has blessed us with every spiritual blessing in the heavenly places in Christ.

EPHESIANS 1:3

❧

God has blessed us "with *every* spiritual blessing." In other words, total blessing. Nothing is missing. If you find that hard to believe or imagine, then notice the all-encompassing words the Bible uses elsewhere when referring to God's gifts to us:

- "His divine power has given to us *all* things that pertain to life and godliness" (2 Peter 1:3).

- "You are *complete* in Him, who is the head of all principality and power" (Colossians 2:10).

- "*Every* good gift and *every* perfect gift is from above and comes down from the Father of lights" (James 1:17).

All. Complete. Every. What more could we want? If we feel we're lacking, maybe we've forgotten some (or many!) of our blessings.

He Is Faithful

Do not worry, saying, "What shall we eat?" or "What shall we drink?" or "What shall we wear?"...For your heavenly Father knows that you need all these things. But seek first the kingdom of God and His righteousness, and all these things shall be added to you.

MATTHEW 6:31-33

❧

Did you know worry and faith are inconsistent? Worry says, in effect, "God, I doubt Your ability to meet my needs." Faith, by contrast, says, "Father, I don't know how You will meet my need, but I know You will."

Here in Matthew 6:31-33, Jesus, the Master Physician, prescribes to us the cure for worry. He tells us to exchange all our earthly distractions for one simple preoccupation: seeking God's kingdom and being right with Him. You mind His business, and He will mind yours.

God's track record speaks for itself. Can we name any of His own whom the Lord has failed to care for? Surely the One who has given us every spiritual blessing in heaven can take care of our every need here on earth.

Fulfillment

The LORD is my shepherd; I shall not want.

PSALM 23:1

Better than a Blank Check

Delight yourself also in the LORD, and He shall give you the desires of your heart.

PSALM 37:4

~

At first glance, this may appear to be a blank check to ask God to give you whatever you want. But it isn't. It's actually better than that. It's an encouragement for you to delight in Him—for your greatest joy to be drawing near to Him and loving Him. And when you do that, you'll find your thoughts, your concerns, and your heart lining up with His. That which is important to God will become important to you.

Drawing near to God will have a profound impact on your desires. God will *want* to fulfill the longings of your heart because they are His longings, too. And you'll be much happier because your yearnings will be for the more noble, more worthy things in life. You'll be living on a much higher plane, seeking those things that have eternal value.

Delight in the Lord...and you won't be disappointed!

No Good Gift Spared

He who did not spare His own Son, but delivered Him up for us all, how shall He not with Him also freely give us all things?

ROMANS 8:32

∾

We could call this the promise of all promises. Here is another way to word it: What can God deny us after having given us Jesus? When God gave us His Son, He gave the greatest gift He could possibly give. In light of that, why would God withhold any lesser gifts from us?

The fact is, He won't. And when He gives, He does so freely. We don't need to force His hand. So if you have a genuine need and bring it before the Lord in prayer, you can be assured He will meet it.

"But I have needs that He hasn't met yet," you say. Consider these possibilities: Does God view your *want* as a true *need*? Might He have delayed His answer till a more appropriate time?

When a "need" goes unmet, may your response be one of trusting God's wisdom rather than doubting His goodness.

Exceedingly Abundantly

*Now to Him who is able to do exceedingly abun-
dantly above all that we ask or think, according to
the power that works in us, to Him be glory.*

EPHESIANS 3:20-21

∽

He is able! As Christians, we have a power at work
within us that can do what we cannot. This wonderful
power is manifest in numerous ways:

God has taken us from spiritual death to spiritual
life. The old man is gone, the new man has come. The
fallen has become the resurrected. That which is mortal
will become immortal. We are being transformed into
the image of Christ. We can now say no to sin and yes
to righteousness. We who were once enemies with God
are now His children. As new creatures, we have new
hearts and minds. We are no longer blind, but have the
Holy Spirit within, enabling us to see clearly and truly
understand God's Word.

And He does so much more for us! Yes, He is able.
His power is unlimited. May we never take His work
in us for granted or fail to thank Him.

Sharing His Riches

The Spirit Himself bears witness with our spirit that we are children of God...and joint heirs with Christ.

ROMANS 8:16-17

౨

Everything that exists in this universe belongs to Christ by divine right. Hebrews 1:2 tells us that God's Son has been "appointed heir of all things." By no means is this limited to the things of this earth; all that is in heaven and the spiritual realm belongs to Him, too.

And because of Christ's work on the cross, in which He took on our unrighteousness and gave us His righteousness, *we are joint heirs with Christ!* That which belongs to Him belongs to us, too. Earthly kings rarely share their wealth with their subjects. By contrast, Christ desires to share all that belongs to Him. We will partake in His honor and riches. We will rule alongside Him, and we will share in His glory.

Second Corinthians 2:8-9 puts it all into perspective for us: "Christ...though He was rich, yet for your sakes He became poor, that you through His poverty might become rich." Have you thanked Him?

Protection

One Almighty is more than all mighties.

WILLIAM GURNALL

Your Great Advocate

If God is for us, who can be against us?

ROMANS 8:31

❧

God guards and protects those who belong to Him. Now, that doesn't mean the path of life will always be smooth. We will encounter people who oppose us and are determined to harm us. Satan will never grow tired of luring us into sin. And notice that James said, "Count it all joy *when* you fall into various trials," not "*if* you fall into various trials." So difficulties and enemies are a certainty for us.

But in the midst of the tough times and persecution, "God is for us." He is our shield, our security, our Protector. God's power to give us victory is greater than any power that might attempt to defeat us. He can overrule all things, and nothing can overrule Him.

God is on your side. He's the greatest advocate you could ever have fighting for you!

A Very Present Help

God is our refuge and strength, a very present help
in trouble.

PSALM 46:1

∽

The words of Psalm 46 inspired Martin Luther to
write the majestic song "A Mighty Fortress Is Our God."
A fortress is appropriate imagery because it portrays
the fact that God is both our refuge *and* our strength.
He provides for us a protective shelter that cannot be
penetrated even in the fiercest of battles, and at the
same time, He equips and empowers us so we can have
strategic advantage over our foes.

God is also a "*very* present help" in trouble. He is
even closer to us than the trouble itself. His availability
to us is instant. With Him, help is never "on the way,"
it's already with us.

As Martin Luther said, "Though this world with
devils filled should threaten to undo us, we will not
fear, for God hath willed His truth to triumph through
us."

Comfort

*The better we understand God's Word,
the more comfort we can find in it;
the darkness of trouble arises from
the darkness of ignorance.*

MATTHEW HENRY

The Wisdom of Waiting on God

I waited patiently for the LORD; and He inclined to me, and heard my cry.

PSALM 40:1

&

Have you ever wished God would hurry up? Sometimes, in our eagerness for results, we run ahead of Him and attempt to make things happen in our own power, without His help. And in the end, the results are never as good as they would have been if we had just waited for God.

Patience is a difficult discipline to cultivate. But it has many benefits. It helps us to check with God first. To wait on His timing. To carefully consider all the alternatives. And to have His divine power at our disposal instead of mere human strength.

Even Jesus waited on God. Early in the morning, He sought God in prayer, waiting for direction and blessing. He had come to do His Father's will, and He paused to make sure He knew what it was before taking action.

Wait...and God will answer.

His Incomparable Care

*Humble yourselves...casting all your care upon Him,
for He cares for you.*

1 PETER 5:6-7

∽

Are you staggering under a weight that your Father in heaven is more than capable of carrying for you? Do you doubt His earnest willingness to help you with the burden that preoccupies you now? Once again, we find within a promise the liberating word "all"! We're to turn *every* concern over to God, regardless of how small it is. The word "casting" means "flinging away"—we are literally commanded to throw our distracting anxieties off our frail shoulders and into His omnipotent hands.

God never intended for us to wear ourselves out over worries. He wants to free us of distractions so we can focus our energies on those things that build up, not weigh down. Repeatedly in the Scriptures, He tells us to rest in Him and not fret.

Resign your problem to Him. *Rest* in His calming grace. And let Him *renew* you by His refreshing power. Give your cares to your Father...and let Him do what only He can do!

He Loves the Unlovely

He heals the brokenhearted and binds up their wounds.

PSALM 147:3

❧

We live in a world that adores the rich and the beautiful, and exalts the strong and the powerful. This has been a problem even within the church—the apostle James had to chastise some believers who were showing favoritism to the rich and disregard for the poor (James 2:1-9).

Yet our high and mighty God chooses to lower Himself and walk among the weak and the wounded. He loves the unlovely and sympathizes with the sick. Few people are willing to spare the time to comfort those whose lives are broken...but God takes special delight in nursing them back to health.

When your life has fallen apart and others have forgotten or abandoned you, your heavenly Father will remain at your side. You will never exhaust His compassions, for they are new every morning. Great is His faithfulness!

The Master Comforter

Praise be to the God and Father of our Lord Jesus Christ, the Father of compassion and the God of all comfort, who comforts us in all our troubles, so that we can comfort those in any trouble with the comfort we ourselves have received from God.

2 CORINTHIANS 1:3-4 (NIV)

❧

Suffering not only drives us closer to God but also equips us to become messengers of comfort and encouragement to others.

If *anyone* can console us, He can...because only He can see clearly into our hearts and minds and understand our need perfectly.

And after we experience His healing touch, we can take what we've learned and pass it along to others who are faced with similar challenges. Such comfort is powerful because we're revealing to others what we learned from the Master Comforter Himself.

So even if you never come to understand why God allowed a certain trial in your life, you're still assured of two unquestionably significant benefits: God will comfort you, and you will then be able to comfort others.

The Promise of a Great Future

God will wipe away every tear from their eyes; there
shall be no more death, nor sorrow, nor crying. There
shall be no more pain, for the former things have
passed away.

REVELATION 21:4

❧

Pain and sorrow are so intertwined into the everyday fabric of our lives that we can't imagine what the
world would be like without them. But consider the
results of pain: Anxiety. Discouragement. Depression.
Grief. Hurt. Bondage. Division. Anger. Bitterness. Empti-
ness. Loss. Darkness. Defeat.

Yet a day is coming when these will pass away, and
we will never experience them again. Instead, we will
know the very best of all God has to offer: Peace. Hope.
Happiness. Joy. Comfort. Freedom. Unity. Love. Sweet-
ness. Fullness. Gain. Light. Victory. And so much more!

The tears we shed—whether from our eyes or in
our heart—will one day be gone, never to come back.
God Himself will wipe them away and usher us into
the new heaven and new earth, into a paradise where
we will never again know sorrow.

Confidence

Assurance...enables a child of God to feel that
the great business of life is a settled business,
the great debt a paid debt,
the great disease a healed disease
and the great work a finished work

J.C. RYLE

A Perfect Track Record

[Abraham] did not waver at the promise of God through unbelief, but was strengthened in faith, giving glory to God, and being fully convinced that what He had promised He was also able to perform.

ROMANS 4:20-21

✎

Even when Abraham was 100 years old and Sarah was 90, Abraham was convinced God would keep His promise that he would have a son and become the father of many nations.

Noah was convinced God would send a worldwide flood and spent 120 years building an ark. Moses was convinced God would set His people free, and he challenged the Pharaoh and all of Egypt.

All through the Bible and across many centuries stretches a long line of saints who were convinced God would keep His promises. And in every instance, God followed through. Not once can we point to a broken promise.

Are you convinced? Or do you waver in unbelief? That which God promises, He *will* perform. His track record is perfect. Rest in His promises...and believe!

God Is Able

My counsel shall stand, and I will do all My pleasure....Indeed I have spoken it; I will also bring it to pass. I have purposed it; I will also do it.

ISAIAH 46:10-11

∽

We can never exhaust the reservoir of God's power or empty the ocean of His strength. Whatever work God begins, He is able to sustain and to complete. Whatever plans He makes, He is able to carry out and achieve. Whatever purpose He establishes, He is able to maintain and accomplish. And whatever promise He utters, He is able to act on and fulfill.

Are you anxious about finding the strength to make it through today? Are you unable to figure out why God has allowed certain things to happen? Are you tempted to question God's purpose? Are you waiting as a promise seems to go unkept?

Remember...God's counsel will stand. Whatever He decides will happen. He will keep you in His plan and purpose, and He will keep His promises. Of this you can be sure: He will never fail you.

Righteousness Will Prevail

*Do not fret because of evildoers, nor be envious of
the workers of iniquity. For they shall soon be cut
down like the grass, and wither as the green herb.*

PSALM 37:1

ᐧᐩᐧ

The Bible repeatedly assures us that God punishes
the wicked and rewards the righteous. But sometimes
we find this hard to believe. Justice is not always
served. The wicked prosper while the righteous suffer.
Why is this so?

We live in a world that chose to reject God's rulership, and because of the Lord's great mercy, He has not
yet taken that rulership back. As He allows evil to run
its course, His desire is that people will see the futility
of their ways and turn to Him. In the meantime, Psalm
37:1 tells us, "Do not fret."

Then we're told the cure for a fretful heart: "Trust
in the LORD, and do good" (verse 3). We're to let God
handle those who do evil while we focus on doing
good.

Someday, righteousness *will* prevail. And when it
does, it will do so for eternity.

Always Providing

I have been young, and now am old; yet I have not seen the righteous forsaken, nor his descendants begging for bread.

PSALM 37:25

❧

One of the Old Testament names for God is Jehovah-Jireh, or "The Lord Will Provide." Taking care of our needs is literally a part of who He is.

Unfortunately, we tend to think of our Father as our provider only in our times of need. For every day that we wonder where our next dollar will come from, we enjoy many days when a dollar is already in hand. For every occasion an unexpected crisis occurs, we see many occasions when all goes smoothly as planned. For every time a circumstance forces us to our knees in prayer, we glide through other times when we don't pray because we see no reason to.

Yet God's providence is as much at work in the less needy times as in the needy. As James 1:17 says, "*Every* good gift and every perfect gift is from above." The more we make an effort to consciously thank God for *everything* at *all* times, the more we will be able to see just how much He really does provide for us.

Answered Prayer

Never was a faithful prayer lost.
Some prayers have a longer voyage than others,
but then they return with their richer lading at last,
so that the praying soul is a gainer by waiting for an answer.

WILLIAM GURNALL

He Hears Your Prayers

This is the confidence that we have in Him, that if we ask anything according to His will, He hears us.

1 JOHN 5:14

&

Embracing the will of God is the highest attainment of prayer. If the petitions we lift up to our heavenly Father are in harmony with His purposes, we can be *fully confident* He will hear them. Of course, He might not answer in the manner or the time that we expect, for He knows the need better than we do, and He will orchestrate His reply to conform to His higher and nobler design for our lives.

How can we ensure that our prayers are "according to His will"?

Keep in mind that we pray not to *inform* God's mind, for He already knows all things even before we ask. We pray not to *change* His mind, for He already has a plan in place and knows what is best. Rather, we pray to *receive* His mind—to ask Him to place His desires in our hearts so we can become cooperative instruments of the work He desires to do on the earth.

Whatever You Ask

*I say to you, whatever things you ask when you pray,
believe that you receive them, and you will have
them.*

MARK 11:24

ை

This seems a very bold statement from Jesus. Does
He literally mean that *whatever* we pray for, we *will*
receive? Anything at all?

First John 5:14 helps complete the picture for us:
"This is the confidence that we have in Him, that if we
ask anything *according to His will*, He hears us." So we
are free to bring our every request...but we must also
realize God always works according to His perfect will
and according to what He knows is best for us. If He
grants our request, He does so because it conforms
with His higher plan and purpose. And when He does
not, His higher love knows what is really better for us.

God would much rather we expand our prayer
requests to Him, allowing Him to teach us through His
yes and no answers, than limit our petitions because we
are unsure of how He might answer. In this way, you
will learn to trust His wisdom.

Blessings Are His Pleasure

Ask, and it will be given to you; seek, and you will find; knock, and it will be opened to you. For everyone who asks receives, and he who seeks finds, and to him who knocks it will be opened.

MATTHEW 7:7-8

❧

Verse 11 sheds even more light on the words above: "If you then, being evil, know how to give good gifts to your children, how much more will your Father who is in heaven give good things to those who ask Him!" In the same way that human parents know their children's needs better than children do, our Father in heaven knows our needs better than we do.

Our Father's storehouse in heaven abounds with blessings for us, and He takes great pleasure in pouring out those blessings on us. That's why He tells us to ask, to seek, to knock. He *wants* our petitions! Yet too often our requests are earthly minded. Or we place constraints on God, telling Him how we expect Him to respond. Instead of limiting Him, or asking amiss, why not give Him a blank check and let Him answer according to His infinite wisdom and grace?

Becoming Mighty in Prayer

If you abide in Me, and My words abide in you, you will ask what you desire, and it shall be done for you.

JOHN 15:7

∽

The key to answered prayer rests on a very big "if"—if you abide in Christ and let His Word abide in you. This abiding means becoming so intimately joined to the Lord that His wishes become yours. As the great English minister C.H. Spurgeon said, "The *carte blanche* can only be given to one whose very life is, 'Not I, but Christ liveth in me.'"

If you wish to be mighty in prayer, Christ must be mighty in you. Jesus confirms this two verses earlier, where He said, "He who abides in Me, and I in him, bears much fruit; for without Me you can do nothing" (verse 5).

Are you abiding in Him? Your honest answer will determine the difference between powerless pleading and powerful praying.

A God Who Hears

The LORD has heard my cry for mercy; the LORD accepts my prayer.

PSALM 6:9 (NIV)

❧

God is a Shepherd who listens with a ready ear for the cries of His sheep. He is ever alert to our pleas for help. He invites us to come before Him with our needs. He is never unavailable or unconcerned. He's eager to care for us, and we need only to remember to come into His presence.

We often try to take life by the horns ourselves. Somehow being tough and self-sufficient seems more virtuous. But we need to remember that our Father's wisdom and strength are infinitely greater than our own and that we have much to gain by seeking His help in every circumstance. May we never hesitate to cry out to Him; may we live in constant readiness to seek Him in prayer...because He *will* listen, and He *will* accept our prayer.

Success

God's definition of success:

"Let not the wise man glory in his wisdom,
let not the mighty man glory in his might,
nor let the rich man glory in his riches;
but let him who glories glory in this,
that he understands and knows Me, that I am the LORD,
exercising lovingkindness, judgment, and righteousness in the
earth. For in these I delight," says the LORD.

JEREMIAH 9:23-24

The Key to Success

This Book of the Law shall not depart from your mouth, but you shall meditate in it day and night, that you may observe to do according to all that is written in it. For then you will make your way prosperous, And then you will have good success.

JOSHUA 1:8

೦ര

What is the connection between applying God's Word to your life and knowing success?

The Bible is like an instruction manual for a technologically complex gadget. When you follow the instructions for usage, the device won't break down or malfunction. And when you adhere to the Bible—the instruction manual for human living—the same is true. As complicated as life is, we need all the help we can get! As A.W. Pink says, "We cannot expect the God of Truth to be with us if we neglect the Truth of God."

Notice that according to Joshua 1:8, merely reading or knowing the Bible is not enough. We are "to *do* according to all that is written in it." Only then can it make a difference *in* us and *through* us and *for* us. Only then will we know success as God defines it.

Leaning on God

*Trust in the L*ORD *with all your heart, and lean not on your own understanding; in all your ways acknowledge Him, and He shall direct your paths.*

PROVERBS 3:5-6

∽

Are you looking for clearer direction in a specific matter? Are you having trouble making a decision? Are you worried about the future? Proverbs 3:5-6 offers good counsel:

Trust Him with all your heart: Do only what you can do, and then leave the results to God. Don't be anxious; trust in the Lord. Worry cannot do anything, but God can do everything.

Lean not on your own understanding: If you can't figure it out, don't try to. Remember, God can see everything, including the future. Lean on *His* understanding.

In all your ways acknowledge Him: That's *all* your ways. Let Him have complete control. Put Him first. Recognize what He can do and has already done.

And He shall direct your paths: When you are fully trusting, fully yielding, and fully honoring God, He can then fully direct your paths.

His Devotion to Us

Because he has set his love upon Me, therefore I will deliver him; I will set him on high, because he has known My name.

PSALM 91:14

◈

Here, God describes the blessings He gives to those who have set their love on Him and know His name. Once again we see the great lengths to which God is eager to shower His grace on us. Our devotion to Him stirs His devotion to us. And what a devotion it is! He promises to deliver us and to set us "on high."

To be set "on high" means to be exalted. How? This can happen as we receive a number of things: a position of honor, a role as a leader, a responsibility as a role model, a stewardship over significant resources, great usefulness or success, special insight or wisdom, or triumph over temptation.

The priority, of course, is our affection for God. Let us not pursue the blessings themselves, but the Lord alone. Then the blessings will come!

Guidance

*In some ways I find guidance, if anything, gets harder
rather than easier the longer I am a Christian.
Perhaps God allows this so that we have to go on
relying on Him and not on ourselves.*

DAVID WATSON

Equipped for Every Good Work

All Scripture is given by inspiration of God, and is profitable for doctrine, for reproof, for correction, for instruction in righteousness, that the man of God may be complete, thoroughly equipped for every good work.

2 TIMOTHY 3:16-17

∞

Why do we have the Bible? So that we can "be complete" and "thoroughly equipped." For what? "*Every good work.*"

Imagine the Bible as sort of a Swiss Army knife—it has all the tools you need to enable your spiritual growth and service. But you can't make use of the Bible if you don't know what it says. The more familiar you are with its contents, the more it can help change your life.

God promises that His Word can equip you for nothing less than *every* good work. If your heart's desire is to be more useful to Him, then put more of His Word in your heart. So "let the word of Christ dwell in you richly" (Colossians 3:16)!

His Promises Stand Forever

Heaven and earth will pass away, but My words will by no means pass away.

MARK 13:31

᷈

When God makes a promise, He guarantees it for eternity. Nothing can void or change His Word. Even if the entire universe were wiped out of existence, His Word would still stand, including all the promises within it.

That should give you some idea of the level of confidence you can place in the Lord's promises. They comprise an anchor that is immovable. A foundation that is unshakeable. A mountain that cannot be toppled.

God's promises can stand forever because He Himself will stand forever. The One who made the promises we've read in this book is infinite. Nothing can limit Him. Therefore, nothing can limit His promises. "There has not failed one word of all His good promise" (1 Kings 8:56). Isn't that incredible?

Make use of His promises. When you do, you will see the mightiness of God on display, as will others. And you'll see just how much He loves you.

Excellent Harvest House
Books on Prayer

THE POWER OF A PRAYING® WIFE

Stormie Omartian. Omartian shares how wives can develop a deeper relationship with their husbands by praying for them. Packed with practical advice on praying for specific areas, including: decision-making, fears, spiritual strength, and sexuality, women will discover the fulfilling marriage God intended.

BRUCE & STAN'S® POCKET GUIDE TO PRAYER

Bruce Bickel and Stan Jantz. This very portable guide to prayer is as fun to read as it is uplifting. Readers will experience the wonder of communicating directly with God as Bruce and Stan explore the truth about how and why to pray.

PRAYING THROUGH THE TOUGH TIMES

Lloyd John Ogilvie. Ogilvie gently guides readers to pray for God's desires! confidence in His nearness; His grace to love others; ability to see with His vision, grasping what the future can be when put in His hands.

A WOMAN'S CALL TO PRAYER

Elizabeth George. Women long for a meaningful prayer life but the demands of family, work, and home can undermine even the best intentions. Elizabeth George, bestselling author and popular teacher, leads women to deeper communication with God.

Inspiring Titles
in the One-Minute Prayers™ Series

ONE-MINUTE PRAYERS™
This collection of simple, heartfelt prayers and Scriptures is designed to serve the place and needs of everyday life. Offering renewal, this prayer journey encourages readers to experience fellowship with God during busy times.

ONE-MINUTE PRAYERS™ FOR BUSY MOMS
Designed to serve the place and needs of everyday life, these simple prayers and inspirational verses are available when needed most. A mother's minute in prayer will free her to find refreshment in God's presence.

ONE-MINUTE PRAYERS™ FOR MEN
These themed, brief prayers draw men to the feet of Jesus where wisdom, direction, and guidance are offered. The format is ideal for businessmen, travelers, and men ready to develop the discipline of prayer.

ONE-MINUTE PRAYERS™ FOR WOMEN
Women who juggle schedules, responsibilities, and commitments will discover sacred moments of renewal among these brief prayers. They will experience the joy of meditation and learn to appreciate their gifts, release guilt, and embrace grace.

ONE-MINUTE PRAYERS™ FOR THOSE WHO HURT
This collection of personal prayers and Scriptures leads the weary to rest during a hectic schedule, directs the lost to God's will during confusing times, and leads the broken to God's mending touch.